# The Creative Collective Anthology

# Series 1

# Contents

1. Society's Perception - Cher Myra – London
2. In the Shadows - Callina Sullivan, Swansea
3. First look - Callina Sullivan, Swansea
4. In Thought - Callina Sullivan, Swansea
5. Deliciously Insane - Emma Reynolds, Poole
6. Lucifers and Gods - Emma Reynolds, Poole
7. Innocence - Emma Reynolds, Poole
8. Lace for Liquorice - Emma Reynolds, Poole
9. The Clown Who Dripped Tears - Emma Reynolds, Poole
10. Cycle - E.O'Brien, Norwich.
11. Fight or Flight - E.O'Brien, Norwich.
12. Soul - E.O'Brien, Norwich.
13. Waves - E.O'Brien, Norwich.
14. Being Three - Joanna H, Southampton
15. Autumn Grey - Joanna H, Southampton
16. Beautiful Butterfly - Joanna H, Southampton
17. George the one eyed Pug - JRB
18. A Love Lost - Amanda P
19. I Wish - Amanda P
20. If There were Icicles on the Moon - Hilary Pinkerton
21. La dama del abanico - Hilary Pinkerton
22. Maria de Rohan - Hilary Pinkerton
23. She - Hilary Pinkerton
24. My Love.... - Hilary Pinkerton
25. Distance - Jarea
26. I Am The Imaginary Tree Of Light - Ninon de Vere De Rosa
27. Sifting Through Our Body Of Passion - Ninon de Vere De Rosa
28. Freedom - Geraldine Taylor
29. Rivers Run - Geraldine Taylor
30. Beloved Has Become - Geraldine Taylor
31. One - Geraldine Taylor
32. Ordained Love - Geraldine Taylor

*A creative collection of poems written by poets from across the globe; as part of an ongoing series.*

## Society's Perception

Society's perception
It's a misinterpretation
No such thing as perfection
This is what causes confliction
Or what causes an addiction
No point in having an expectation
This is what causes dysfunction
Or even affiliation
Why not stick together as a nation?
Have less frustration
But more concentration
Make life a celebration
Instead of a contradiction
Cut out the frustration
Focus on the inspiration
To attract fascination
Provide a lot of information
To cause negotiation
Everyone deserves recognition
Because in this world there's restriction
Like tough rules on immigration
Working in an institution
This all causes segregation
Sometimes even suffocation
It's time to end this misconception
And stop this suppression
Start achieving satisfaction
Everyone has a passion
So stop giving into temptation
Or believing everything on television
Have a positive and realistic vision
Then put things into action

Cher Myra – London

## In the Shadows

In darkness, a footstep.
An echo.
He stops to listen.
Empty.

One step forward,
Towards the light,
The shadows reaching for him
With all their might.

He runs,
Faster now,
No-one behind.
Faster, faster towards the safe glow.

Breathing hard,
He slows his pace,
No-one behind,
Nobody there.

One more step,
He reaches the light,
A deep breath, calm,
He hates walking at night.

Callina Sullivan, Swansea

**First look**

A look for the first time,
I gaze into your eyes,
Both bewildered,
A little afraid,

Will I be strong enough for what you will bring?
A lifetime of loving and caring for you,
In my arms, a bundle of joy.

Of sleepless nights and lots of cries,
But all will be worth it,
You'll know it one day.

I'll keep you safe
As I watch you grow,
Into a little girl,
A woman,
My own.

For Ruby.

Callina Sullivan, Swansea

**In Thought**

Looking to the skies, grey and gloomy,
I wonder what hope there is.

Clouds so heavy, a burden on my soul,
I feel the sadness of many.

Up in the sky, a bird passes by,
Is that you up there?

There, a glint, a shimmer of sun,
The hope springs back to mind.

In one small ray, I remember your smile,
That'll brighten each thought for today.

Callina Sullivan, Swansea

## Deliciously Insane

Gently the broken keys of the piano begin to play,
Humming a melody of suffocated youth, it rings in my ears,
As if the ice cold snow of old had melted and gone away,
As if the pounding heat of the sun had begun to enter back into my years.

Beautifully the pale skin of virginity and love bled into a sick want,
Innocence sprawled across the floor like death in paradise,
Deafeningly repeating its lustful taunt,
A child turned woman knew a symphony would no longer suffice.

Her soul churning into a fiery globe of influence,
His soul imploding with devilish delight,
Whimsical minds blew away her precious prudence,
All was left was that shining white light.

Illuminating the personal shapes of her,
Attacking and invading every internal secret she bare,
Untrustworthy like the Lucifers that were,
Along with the wind flew the essence of her care.

Slicing at any morals that remained,
Scratching at any emotion the weak heart could squeeze into existence,
Her brain spun, wonderfully pained,
Giving into every command of his persistence.

Love was suddenly a memory of fairy tales,
This child was deliciously trapped in the gaze of an ogre,
Amazingly he was calling and she was the delicate princess that trails,
His poison from there on made her spit crushed vulgarity, you could not separate her from that who owned her.

Grace and amazement was left in the triumph of church steeples,
Respect and decorum was shunned into the disrespect of the dark alleys,
Musky and tainted perfumes filled rooms from masses of peoples,
Blood spread through the serenity of pure valleys.

She was deliciously insane.

Emma Reynolds, Poole

## Lucifers and Gods

When the Crimson skies are dimming low,
And the mountains of peace are crumbling away,
A bird of paradise emerges to lead you where to go,
To the place where beauty and admiration lay.

A hand as large as God's gently caresses you,
Placing you on a pedestal cloud high above,
You grow with Him and become powerful too,
This love becoming pure as the soaring dove.

The gentle blue of the morn does not remain,
And the assassination of the sun is brought when the thunder comes,
Your happiness and joy is lost in the flood of the rain,
And petrifying roars over-bare your once gentle hums.

Trapped in unrighteous pain and broken dreams,
Your lesser God drifts like smoke into the flames of deceit,
The pure Angel of beauty was dying it seems,
And not one Lucifer reflected the God that she wanted to meet.

Emma Reynolds, Poole

**Innocence**

Wall Street was booming like a bomb hit New York City,
People were scurrying about the town in a buzz so busy.
This was a new era for the Big Apple,
This was a city for the extraordinary and able.

Celebrities from far and wide came to awe at the view,
Boats would sail and you would boggle at the crew,
Actors, singers, the great Bank Broker,
The nights would flash by in a spin and a whir.

Liquor was cheaper than ever before,
And the public was yearning for more and more,
Parties were going on till dawn,
And adult deers were created from the innocence of a fawn.

The high life was great until one night,
When I lost my innocence in an eerie fight,
Four months later a bump appeared,
And I began to drown in my bitter tears.

To remove the ball was not legal,
And I was too far gone to be left stable,
The baby was kept; it was a little girl,
Her life began to unfurl.

The price I paid was too painful,
But my beautiful girl was born in April.
She was beautiful as a rose,
No matter how her life was chose.

Take me back to the days of partying and alcohol,
Where I could take a midnight stroll,
Have no care or false pretense,
Just pure love and innocence.

Emma Reynolds, Poole

# Lace for Liquorice

His mouth pressed into a thin line,
Straight through me his piercing black eyes stared,
He reassured me everything would be just fine,
Never before had I been so scared.

A grimacing look but accompanied by allure,
The whisky and smoke stained room was filled with tension,
I was dressed up all for him, the latest fashion in lace couture,
He promised black lies no innocent mouth could mention.

He was sticky just like liquorice,
His God like hands controlling the pure creature beneath him,
The silk sheets were splattered with filth as the night became feverish,
The love she wanted didn't appear, the shining sun grew dim.

Crumbled like a handkerchief thrown from his pocket she lay down,
Falling to the floor her golden hair shivered in the breeze,
Still beautiful she belonged to him in that crushed velvet gown,
Dripping in red she poured out for him, his own personal tease.

Arranging the lapel of his tailored suit,
He leaves for a moment to fly off into the neon night,
All she can contemplate is her violation from a brute,
As she lay there slung on the chaise long and blinded herself to his cheated sight.

Emma Reynolds, Poole

**The Clown Who Dripped Tears**

He looks in the mirror with a nasty taste,
Picks up a tissue and wipes the makeup off of his face.
A lessoned reminder of a familiar smile,
No one could have guessed this man was on trial.

Every night he walked into the circus crypt,
The crowd would laugh as he comically tripped,
Around the arena, many had seen him,
Pulling off the familiar faked grin.

The circus is over,
It's time to go sir,
Here is your pay clown,
Aren't you meant to smile, not frown?

A frown is what sat on his lips,
Even now with a hat full of tips,
Because he was a drunken extraordinary lad,
Who regretted gambling everything his heart had had.

So now as he sat there in a glowing boudoir,
He debated whether home or bar,
The clown chose neither, for of course he had told her,
That he could never make it that far.

The clown never made it at all in fact,
This was his best and last act,
Never would he perform again,
He was not an asset to what they called man.

So when he was found the day after,
By a girlfriend he used to delight with happiness and laughter,
He was completely dead, who'd of knew?
People had realised the clown had feelings and lost all track of what to think and do.

A suicide note, left on the desk, read:
Sorry my sweet, I know you see me dead.
I never wished this for you.
But in the end what could I do? I had betrayed you. Know none but a few, of this tale dirty but true.

I done you a wrong dear,
I knew you would soon hear,
Of my act of adultery,
And if you knew, we would be through, then, who would I be?

Emma Reynolds, Poole

**Cycle**

Taking up the sun and sand,
He comes and takes you by the hand.
Spinning movements, throwing motions,
Soon, you'll find abhorrent commotion.

He takes you by the soul and pulls,
He delves into your beautiful.
Soon, in time you've come to find,
Bricked walls, and pairs of eyes.
They've come to see the waves inside.
To view forbidden, fruitful, beautiful lands,
Become obliterated, by corrosive hands.

E.O'Brien, Norwich.

## Fight or Flight

Looking upon your face is like staring into a dragons gaze,
I don't know if you'll soar with me or set me ablaze.
Protect me fiercely, I need your faith,
For I can soften your need for fury and flames.
Yet if you bolt furiously, fly to lands afar,
I'll lose the entire meaning,
For my hearts beating.
You'll see you soared away all too soon,
There is no other who will love you like I do.
Tears roll down my cheeks as unwanted reminders of seeing you.
Blinded to your hearts bleeding need for a humans being to soothe you,
You push me down just to see what you smother,
Wrestle your own beast and treasure your lover.
Fly for your beauty but come back to me.
We soared together once and that's where we should eternally be.
Dragon soul and mother warrior need each other.
When we ignited, our eyes did become one, insighted.
For all that we've done, I cannot allow it to be in vain,
I'll bear the fear of flame, the thought of flight,
But I cannot bare the way you stare at me with disdain.
It's probably better for now you leave me today,
Every fiber of my being wants you to be mine......
But every surge of brain power, is telling you to fly.

E.O'Brien, Norwich.

**Soul**

There will come a day when the moon and sun I see,
Will be replaced with space stretching infinitely.
With cosmic swirls filled of lands, stars and trees,
Waterfalls, sand and seas.
But I won't be there anymore,
My vessel bound there forever more,
My essence part of the ether that's flying further on.

Levitating in boundless time,
With all knowledge I have in mind.
Staring at the creator and created,
That flows together in perfect unison.
Watching waves of particles,
Making separate articles of us all.
The continuing continuum continues on through each of us all,
Set to forget this, after each and every one.

The circle of life _
Collides with time and winds back on.
Through a portal of light, that in time,
Portrays all that you could ever find.
Right now, in this moment, I know that I belong.

Then, a voice in the back of me says;
You'll be back around somewhere,
We will meet again; when you come and join in this end.
Next time, I pray you stay with me,
Where there's no obstacles of ourselves to defend.

For now I see,
So True and clearly;
There is no journey's end.....

E.O'Brien, Norwich.

**Waves**

Blackness, grey static, quick sand.
Stuck; with no one's hand.
This crushing, bitter, static evokes a cascading wave of inner no man's land,
I crawl to my fetal ball,
To pretend there are no suffocating claustrophobic white wash walls.
Every second is like a chalkboard being clawed,
The silence speaking to me,
All the things that haunt me.....will never be.


He enters his tormented inner monologue of ego monster and humbled hero,
While he wears the stare of a corpse.

I cry for the wasted time.
How the eyes of his being,
Decided to not see,
Even though to deny my truths speaking,
Was to kill what future was for seen.

What does it matter now?

I was right there....not keen to be unseen.

Miles from me, slipping,
You smother your tears as you go toe to toe with your inner demon,
While outwardly demonstrating how your experience of human has lost all feeling.

Stuck here, I hold my pain in,
While crushing waves cascade over,
Slamming me against white walls.
Laying, the light of my ceiling,
I've stared at for countless hours,
Trying to find the answers to it all.
After a while, you go to that place I envy and despise,
Where you feel nothing at all,
Like a ghostly sunrise.

I use to see you on the other side of no man's land,
Now we are world's apart and I don't know you anymore.
You're lost down there, I'm trapped in here.

Both pacing like frantic lions in a rage,
Madness and fear flooding outwardly,
Spilling between the bars of the cage.

E.O'Brien, Norwich.

**Being Three**

Being Three
Is everything I thought it would be
It's so much better than two
There's so many more things to do
You can walk a lot more
You can even say things you couldn't before
I feel I'm much bigger
So much more mature
I just can't wait till I'm going on four
I know I'm a little person
But, I'm growing up fast
I'm making the most of it
As I know it won't last
Being three

Joanna H, Southampton

**Autumn Grey**

As the autumn sun
Warms through the cold trees like a torch
The dew lays like a carpet of glitter
As I gaze from my porch
Tiny ice sprinkled like scattered crystals
Upon sodden ground
Twisted brances, bare, pointing their
Fingers to the free fields of the sky
No leaves to be found
The pond with its mirror-top glaze
The air full of damp moist haze
Cold day, wonderful day
As silver rain falls
On autumn grey

Joanna H, Southampton

## Beautiful Butterfly

Beautiful butterfly don't fade in my hand
A while ago you were flying the land
Dancing around flowers the pond and sun light
With your delicate wings so pretty and bright
Go play around the garden with others like you
And do all the things that butterflies do
The sky is there to explore like a kite
But all you do is sit there with your wings closed up tight
Beautiful butterfly
Is this your last flight
Then I'll put you somewhere safe
And bid you goodnight

Joanna H, Southampton

**George the one eyed Pug**

Pugs may come and Pugs may go and most just pass you by
Then suddenly along comes George... and he's only got one eye!
'He's only got one eye?' folk say in some surprise
Was he born that way? they want to know, with only half his eyes?
Black as night he lost his sight to a cat with swift sharp claws
But he does alright with his single sight... apart from walking into doors.

JRB

**A love lost**

So you say am special and you say you care
But you're out playing about, your just not there.
Your love is empty it's lost in your fickle heart.
Can't u see your driving us apart .

Well I'm not listening not no more!
Soon i'll be walking out that door.
I'm gonna start again find someone new .
You can't go on treating me as you do .

I need love that makes my heart beat in time with the songs .
I want a love that believes in me where I belong .
I don't want a one, a one sided love affair .
I will find the one and that special love to share !! .

Amanda P

**I wish**

To hear your voice, to feel your kiss
To burn under your touch, is what I wish .
I wish you'd kiss me from head to toe,
I wish for your tongue to tease me real slow .
I wish I could trace  your every contour  your every line,
I wish for your body lying close next to mine.
I want us to be entangled and entwined,
I want me to be forever on your mind. .

Amanda  P

## If there were Icicles on the Moon

If there were icicles on the moon
I could not love you too soon
You are my rock
The hands on the clock
Which turn so slowly
As you are below me
You are above me
You cry so shyly
I love you
Forever

Hilary Pinkerton

**La dama del abanico by Velázquez**

Slow, burning beauty
Slower love is my duty
Handsome face, handsome breast
Womanly wile *will* not me rest
Quiet eyes, but quiet not
The fan is foil to sultry hot
Ash-white skin, blackened cloth
Your fixéd mien is my death

And your closéd lips do say
Wait for me, until the day…..

Hilary Pinkerton

## Maria de Rohan

Red'ning beauty, mine to touch
Damask rose, glories such
Your easy pride withers me
Fallen Love, mine to be
My happy joys are all around
While Deadly Death makes no sound…..

Hilary Pinkerton

**She**

While the bending bough does break
She calls me from my sleep awake
While I stir from afar
She watches from her wan'dring star
While I seek not to know
She the dandelion does blow

And all of this I see in her
While I hard try not to care…..

A name as simple as…..*She*

Hilary Pinkerton

**My Love….**

A scarecrow
Birds peck my eyes
My flat eyes
Full of misery
Raw
With blood tears
Her hair is violets
Mine is filth
Rose-filth
The sky is my living death
The sun is black
The moon is white as my Lover's hand
Which does not touch my cheek.

Hilary Pinkerton

**Distance**

It ain't about the distance, I can go the distance knock on your door I conquered the distance. Hop on a plane get there in an instant. Made it this far cause of my persistence. Throw me the line, pour me some wine, engage in the convo while we fine dine. Ain't standing on the sidelines normal life guidelines walk by my side cause it's time to outshine. Star of the year 5 letters on the big sign.

Social media reverbnation and it's all mine. Ever feel depressed just call that downtime push that aside Jarea be the headline. Photo shoot going down looking so fine. Celebrated to the max got my own shrine. Ain't afraid to chill with the stars, dance with the stars cause I flew very far. Moddish rap that's what I discard bring a new sound that's how I play the part. Here for the taking never gonna depart. The rhythm and the rhymes are never apart. Euphony and ballad coming from the heart.

Jarea

## I Am The Imaginary Tree Of Light

As the mind floats into its fantasy world of passion and takes over the lonely tree that stands
in all its glory with its glowing gown preparing to be undressed as each leaf floats away to the
sound of music to a place of no return; the cold winter days of rain and wind take over and
slowly leaf by leaf undresses the tree of beauty and becomes a naked body.

I toss and turn and in my imaginary mind I see the tree as a passionate naked body searching
for life, my hands become branches and intertwine with the forgotten tree caressing each branch
letting it know you are no longer alone in a world of passion that the tranquility of love has
taken over, embracing it's wish to no longer be that naked lonely tree:

As the light slowly seeks in followed by the wind and warmth of the day I feel the soft hands
embracing each branch, being caressed with passion and love as the buds are forming.
The imaginary mind looks at the tree blossoming in all its glory with its new gown
for the world to see. I am no longer a naked tree. "I Am The Imaginary Tree Of Light"….

Ninon de Vere De Rosa

**Sifting Through Our Body Of Passion**

As I touch the surface of life a thought captures my mind of gravity and I push away the tears of no reason or compassion.
I sink into my world that I only dream of through my fantasized mind and brain that never stops thinking of my next desire...
Like a drop of perfume that belongs to no one and yet falls into my brain of thought that will take me to a place of everlasting desire.

With anticipation of the mind as the perfume grows weaker and weaker and the moment is getting closer, trying to control the
brain to a coherent place at the twist of a voice that runs through my head and the body becomes out of control as the voice goes
deeper in to my skin and out through my hands as they caress his untouchable body and float over his skin like silk we rise together.

As my body awakens to the soft sound of music, feeling the vibration running through my helpless mind taking me out of control
and bringing the touch that only music can give the comfort. Extracting every part of our human control into a helpless state of mind
and body; leaving us with nothing we cannot explain, braking down in a helpless way of desire and passion... "Sifting Through Our Body Of Passion"

Ninon de Vere De Rosa

# Freedom

Unhampered velocity, flow of continuity
Selected autonomy, explore your philosophy
Treaded geography, to grasp empathically
Of no ambiguity, to reason amicably
Of no accord, nonsensical
The freedom just to be

Desire ambitiously, of difference unusually
Give access academically, promotions periodically
Acts of kind sporadically, improvise remarkably
Caring sentimentally, peacefulness tranquillity
Of one accord intentional
The freedom to be me

Geraldine Taylor

## Rivers Run

Rivers run, rivers flow, let it flow, let it flow
Creativity, never let it go
The bud that must flower, the tree that must grow
Seeds of germination, future take shape
Tis the dreamers, the believers, the doers, the achievers
Who so create tomorrow's world
The missionaries, the visionaries, a land of oysters, a sea of pearls
For they are the exceptions to the norm
Of no measure to conform
The beacons of light, with wings they take flight
Inner propensity, with authenticity, they make it a priority
To shape society, and so establish, their mark in history
They venture beyond the comfort zone, a road less travelled
If so alone
Camouflaged not, born to stand out
To realize within, manifest without
Captains of their destiny, they pave the way for others to be
Purpose, passion, legacy, extraordinaire, epitome
Yet beyond limits, illusions overcome
Great beyond measure, their rule of thumb
Multi-dimensional, that which was chose
The vessels of which creativity flows
The journey of life, taken at the helm
With access to another realm
Transcendent thought, that cannot be bought
Noteworthy cause, lest run-of-the-mill
Guided forward by a higher will

Geraldine Taylor

**Beloved Has Become**

To see beyond sight, a vision of the night
Of eyes that would amaze, the stillness of your gaze
Windows of your soul, capture and behold
Delighteth thee

Ever-crescent moon, of harmony in tune
The dawning of the sun, beloved has become
Enlighten me

Enduring to remain, the fire to my flame
Stellar all the while, an enigmatic smile
Rooted ever deeper, devotion of a keeper
Embrace me lest I f
                   a
                     l
                       l
My confidant, my all

Geraldine Taylor

**One**

The one who stands beyond compare

Evolving days of which to share

Of whom I call to reminisce

Allied shoulder greatest bliss

Depths of all transparency

Of cares transferred especially

Leading steps of harmony

Gazes fixed observably

Seeketh not, that which was found

Tested time of ways abound

Dearest truly, purposed for

Sailed me forth beyond the shore

As the other significantly

Won my heart victoriously

If ever there was a love that's true

Of such I always found in you


Geraldine Taylor

## Ordained Love

There is a bountiful harvest, enriched with all love
Where the mysteries of life connect from above
A season of promise, with rivers that flow
From the highest mountain, to the waters below

Abound in all joy, with reverence divine
Proceed to the place where souls intertwine
A threefold cord, yet two souls unite
With endless love, to the Father's delight

An enchanted rose, be granted to thee
Your dearly beloved, embraced splendidly
A foundation in God, a new gift of peace
A trust in his will, where all doubt will cease

The promise of God, the call of his command
Trust and be held in the palm of his hand
A covenant made, the exchanging of rings
Soaring upon these enchanted wings

Cherish therein, the dreams of each other
Exemplify a bond that few will discover
A solemn vow, new mercies to see
An honour established with humility

To have and to hold and welcome each other
An honourable day embracing each other
Proclaim the goodness that comes from above
May the both of you continue in love

Geraldine Taylor

*Created by Geraldine Taylor*

*Ambassador - Author - Poet - Songwriter - Spoken Word Artist*

# Created by Geraldine Taylor ©

Printed in Great Britain
by Amazon